JOY COMES IN THE MOURNING

"For his anger endureth but a moment; in his favour is life: weeping may endure for a night, but joy cometh in the morning."
- Psalm 30:5

A 31-DAY GRIEF DEVOTIONAL & WORKBOOK

Lawanda Walker -Tave

ACKNOWLEDGEMENT:

TO MY LORD AND SAVIOUR, JESUS CHRIST FOR HIS UNCONDITIONAL LOVE AND UNSPEAKABLE GIFT OF SALVATION.

TO ANDREW, FOR HIS CONSTANT SUPPORT AND UNENDING LOVE.

TO MY CHILDREN, JAYDEN AND LYRIAH FOR THE CONSTANT HAPPINESS AND JOY YOU BRING TO MY LIFE.
IT'S MY ULTIMATE HONOR TO BE CALLED YOUR MOTHER.

TO MY PASTOR ROBERT GRAY II, THANK YOU FOR YOUR SPIRITUAL GUIDANCE FOR SO MANY YEARS.

TO TWO OF MY BEST FRIENDS
BLESSITT AND ELIZABETH THANK YOU FOR YOUR SUPPORT ON THIS JOURNEY.

LAWANDA WALKER-TAVE IS A COMPASSIONATE WIFE, DEDICATED MOTHER, AND PASSIONATE ADVOCATE FOR MENTAL HEALTH AND WELL-BEING. BORN AND RAISED IN HENDERSON, TX, LAWANDA'S JOURNEY THROUGH LIFE'S CHALLENGES LED HER TO DISCOVER HER CALLING IN SUPPORTING OTHERS THROUGH THEIR OWN STRUGGLES. WITH A HEART FULL OF EMPATHY AND A DEEP UNDERSTANDING OF THE HUMAN EXPERIENCE, SHE HAS DEVOTED HER CAREER TO GUIDING INDIVIDUALS TOWARDS HEALING AND EMPOWERMENT.

CURRENTLY RESIDING IN LONGVIEW, TX, LAWANDA FINDS INSPIRATION IN HER ROLES AS A DEVOTED WIFE TO ANDREW AND A LOVING MOTHER TO HER CHILDREN, JORDAN, LYRIAH, AND JAYDEN. HER PERSONAL EXPERIENCES WITH GRIEF AND LOSS HAVE FUELED HER MISSION TO HELP OTHERS NAVIGATE THEIR OWN JOURNEYS OF OVERCOMING ADVERSITY AND FINDING HOPE AMIDST DESPAIR.

LAWANDA'S APPROACH TO OVERCOMING GRIEF IS ROOTED IN EMPATHY, RESILIENCE, AND FAITH. DRAWING FROM HER EXPERTISE AS A GRIEVING MOTHER, SHE PROVIDES PRACTICAL STRATEGIES, HEARTFELT INSIGHTS, AND PROFOUND WISDOM TO GUIDE READERS TOWARDS HEALING AND RENEWAL. THROUGH HER WRITING, LAWANDA OFFERS A BEACON OF LIGHT FOR THOSE TRAVERSING THE DARK TUNNELS OF GRIEF, REMINDING THEM THAT THEY ARE NOT ALONE AND THAT THERE IS HOPE ON THE HORIZON.

WITH HER DEBUT SELF-HELP BOOK, LAWANDA WALKER-TAVE INVITES READERS TO EMBARK ON A TRANSFORMATIVE JOURNEY TOWARDS HEALING, RESILIENCE, AND INNER PEACE. HER WORDS RESONATE WITH AUTHENTICITY AND GRACE, OFFERING SOLACE AND INSPIRATION TO ALL WHO SEEK COMFORT IN THE MIDST OF LIFE'S STORMS.

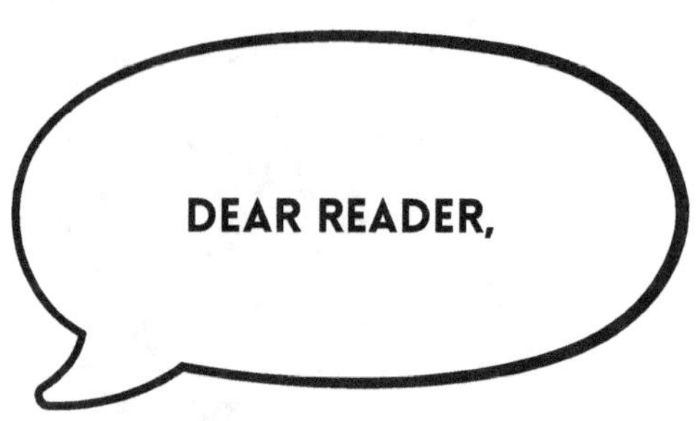

WHETHER YOU ARE ON DAY 1 , 6 MONTHS, OR 10 PLUS
YEARS IN YOUR GRIEF JOURNEY THERE IS SOMETHING
IN THIS BOOK, THAT WILL HELP YOU AND STRENGTHEN YOU
TO KEEP MOVING FORWARD.
IN THE MIDST OF GRIEF, IT CAN BE HARD TO SEE A WAY FORWARD.
WHILE I WAS WRITING, THIS BOOK BECAME A THERAPEUTIC
JOURNEY FOR ME. WITH EACH CHAPTER
OFFERING VALUABLE INSIGHTS AND HELPING ME BECOME
INCREASINGLY STRONGER IN MY WALK THROUGH GRIEF.
GRIEF MAY BE A CONSTANT COMPANION FOR SOME OF US,
BUT IT DOESN'T HAVE TO DEFINE WHO WE ARE COMPLETELY.

YOURS TRULY,
LAWANDA WALKER-TAVE

PONDER THE MOMENT
"LUKE 2:19"

I WOKE UP FEELING

| AWESOME | GOOD | OKAY | NOT GOOD | HORRIBLE |

MEMORIZE THE DEFINITION OF GRIEF:

GRIEF- DEEP SORROW, ESPECIALLY THAT CAUSED BY SOMEONE'S DEATH.

KEY FACTS ABOUT GRIEF:

1.) GRIEF IS A RESPONSE TO THE LOSS OF SOMEONE OR SOMETHING THAT WAS IMPORTANT.

2.) GRIEF CAN OCCUR AFTER A DEATH, DIVORCE, ILLNESS, OR OTHER LOSSES. .

3.) GRIEF CAN AFFECT YOUR PHYSICAL, MENTAL, AND SPIRITUAL HEALTH.

4.) THE GRIEF EXPERIENCE IS DIFFERENT FOR EVERYONE.

5.) THERE MAY BE SECONDARY LOSSES TO DEAL WITH ALSO.

WHAT DOES GOD SAY ABOUT GRIEF?

PSALM 34:15
"THE EYES OF THE LORD ARE UPON THE RIGHTEOUS AND HIS EARS ARE OPEN UNTO THEIR CRY."

PONDER THE MOMENT
"LUKE 2:19"

PONDER THE MOMENT

"LUKE 2:19"

PONDER THE MOMENT
"LUKE 2:19"

I WOKE UP FEELING

AWESOME   **GOOD**   **OKAY**   **NOT GOOD**   **HORRIBLE**

THERE ARE 5 STAGES OF GRIEF :

1.) DENIAL- FEELING NUMB IS COMMON IN THE EARLY DAYS OF AFTER DEATH. SOME PEOPLE CARRY ON AS IF NOTHING HAPPENED EVEN WHEN WE KNOW IN OUR HEADS THAT SOMEONE HAS DIED. IT CAN BE HARD TO BELIEVE THAT THEY ARE NOT COMING BACK.

2.) ANGER- IS A NATURAL EMOTION. DEATH SEEMS UNFAIR ESPECIALLY WHEN WE FEEL THAT SOMEONE HAS DIED BEFORE THEIR TIME. SOMETIMES WE CAN FEEL ANGRY TOWARDS THE PERSON WHO HAS DIED.

3.) BARGAINING-IS WHEN WE START TO MAKE DEALS WITH OURSELVES OR EVEN WITH GOD. HOPING THAT IF WE ACT A CERTAIN WAY GOD WILL SEND OUR LOVED ONE BACK.UNFORTUNATELY THINGS DON'T WORK LIKE THAT .

4.) DEPRESSION - SADNESS, HOPELESSNESS, AND LONGING ARE WHAT WE THINK OF THE MOST OFTEN WHEN GRIEVING. DEPRESSION CAN BE PAINFUL AND INTENSE AND CAN ALSO COME IN WAVES AT ANY GIVEN MOMENT.

5. ACCEPTANCE-GRIEF COMES AND GOES AND IT FEELS LIKE NOTHING WILL, EVER BE THE SAME. OVERTIME THE PAIN DOES EASE UP BUT DOESN'T END. WE MAY NEVER "GET OVER" THE DEATH OF OUR LOVED ONE. BUT DON'T FEAR YOU WILL LEARN TO LIVE AGAIN.

WHAT STAGE ARE YOU IN? ____________________

____

MATTHEW 5:4
"BLESSED ARE THEY THAT MOURN:
FOR THEY SHALL BE COMFORTED. "

PONDER THE MOMENT
"LUKE 2:19"

PONDER THE MOMENT
"LUKE 2:19"

PONDER THE MOMENT
"LUKE 2:19"

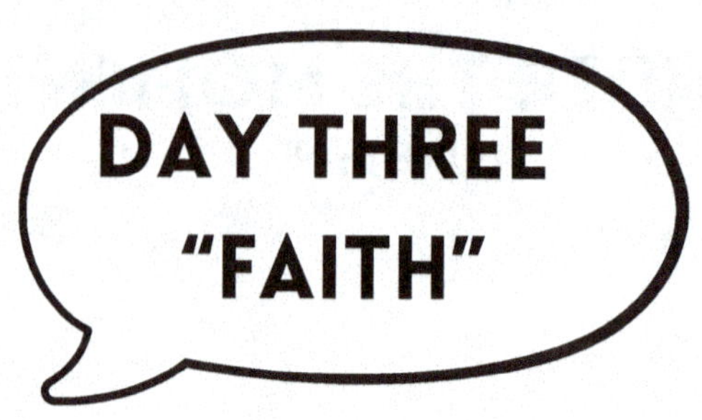

I WOKE UP FEELING

| AWESOME | GOOD | OKAY | NOT GOOD | HORRIBLE |

FAITH–IS A PERSONAL MEASUREMENT OF THE LEVEL OF CONFIDENCE IN WHAT CHRIST HAS DONE AND WILL DO IN, THROUGH AND FOR US.

WHAT DOES FAITH MEAN TO YOU WHILE TRAVELING THROUGH GRIEF?

"WHEN WE ARE FACED WITH A LIFE EVENT SUCH AS DEATH. OUR FAITH CAN BE PULLED TOWARDS EITHER THE LOSS OF FAITH OR THE STRENGTHENING OF OUR FAITH."

HOW HAS FAITH HELPED YOU ON THIS GRIEF JOURNEY?

PONDER THE MOMENT
"LUKE 2:19"

PONDER THE MOMENT
"LUKE 2:19"

PONDER THE MOMENT
"LUKE 2:19"

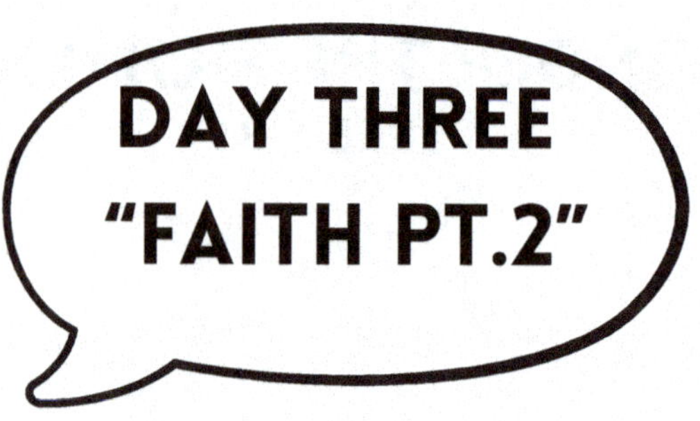

I WOKE UP FEELING

| AWESOME | GOOD | OKAY | NOT GOOD | HORRIBLE |

NAME 3 GREAT CHARACTERISTICS OF FAITH. MATTHEW 15:21-28

1.)

2.)

3.)

"HOW TO EXCHANGE YOUR HURT FOR FAITH"

YOU MUST LIFT YOU EYES HIGHER AND UNDERSTAND THAT LIFE IS TEMPORAL, AND ETERNITY IS FOREVER. WE ALSO WILL NEED TO SURRENDER OUR PRESENT, PAST, AND FUTURE HURTS TO GOD. WHEN WE GIVE THEM TO GOD IT RELEASES THE PAIN FROM US. IT ALSO MAKES ROOM FOR GOD TO HEAL OUR HURTS.
HAVING FAITH MEANS FINDING PEACE IN UNCERTAINTY.

YOU CAN'T ALWAYS TRACE GOD, BUT YOU CAN ALWAYS TRUST GOD!!
KEEP THE FAITH!!

HEBREWS 11:1
"NOW FAITH IS THE SUBSTANCE OF THINGS HOPED FOR, THE EVIDENCE OF THINGS NOT SEEN."

PONDER THE MOMENT
"LUKE 2:19"

PONDER THE MOMENT
"LUKE 2:19"

PONDER THE MOMENT
"LUKE 2:19"

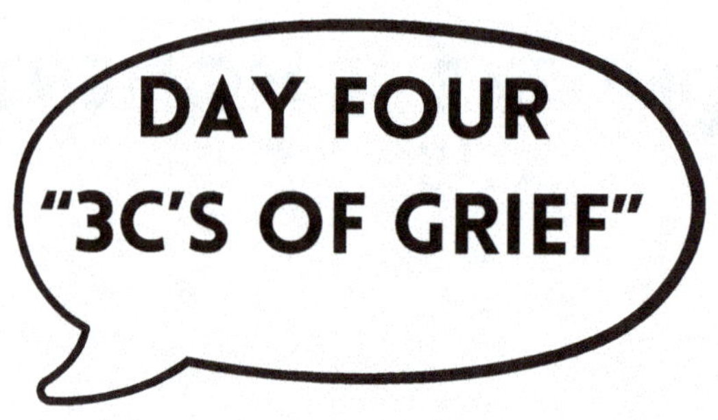

I WOKE UP FEELING

AWESOME   GOOD   OKAY   NOT GOOD   HORRIBLE

**REMEMBERING AND
PRACTICING THE 3C'S OF GRIEF:**

1.) CHOOSE, CONNECT, AND COMMUNICATE

> EVEN DURING THESE DARK MOMENTS OF GRIEF. YOU
> STILL HAVE THE POWER TO CHOOSE, CONNECT, AND
> COMMUNICATE FOR YOURSELF.

THE GRIEF JOURNEY ISN'T A SPRINT; IT'S MORE LIKE A MARATHON.
JUST LIKE MOST TRACK RUNNERS, WE WILL NOT GET THROUGH
OUR GRIEF IN 5 MINUTES, OR 5 MONTHS AND
WE NEED TO BE OK WITH THAT.

WHAT ARE YOU GRATEFUL FOR TODAY?

JOHN 14:1
"LET NOT YOUR HEART BE TROUBLED: YE BELIEVE
IN GOD, BELIEVE ALSO IN ME."

PONDER THE MOMENT

"LUKE 2:19"

PONDER THE MOMENT
"LUKE 2:19"

PONDER THE MOMENT
"LUKE 2:19"

I WOKE UP FEELING

AWESOME   GOOD   OKAY   NOT GOOD   HORRIBLE

SELF- CARE DAY

A SELF-CARE DAY IS A REGULAR COMMITMENT TO SET ASIDE TIME FOR THINGS THAT WILL HELP YOU TO RECHARGE, REFRESH, AND REJUVENATE YOUR LIFE.

6 AREAS OF SELF-CARE

1.) INTELLECTUAL
2.) ENVIRONMENTAL

3.) FINANCIAL
4.) SPIRITUAL

5.) PHYSICAL
6.) MENTAL.

WHAT DID YOU DO FOR YOU TODAY?

- PAUSE AND BREATHE
- JOURNALING
- BIBLE READING
- READ A BOOK
- DO A CRAFT
- COOK A FAVORITE MEAL

WHAT ARE YOU THANKFUL FOR TODAY....

PONDER THE MOMENT

"LUKE 2:19"

PONDER THE MOMENT
"LUKE 2:19"

PONDER THE MOMENT
"LUKE 2:19"

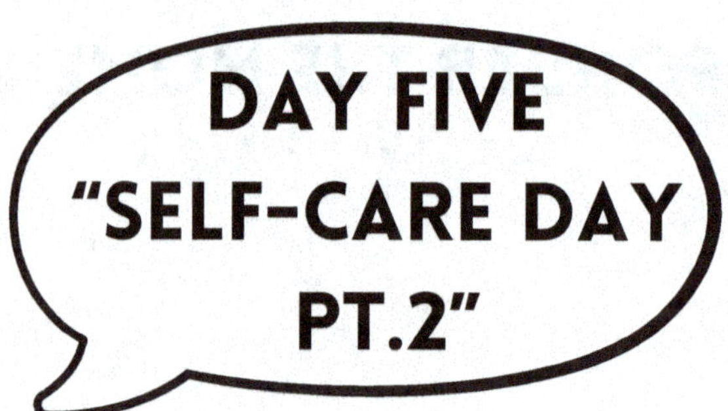

I WOKE UP FEELING

 AWESOME  GOOD  OKAY  NOT GOOD  HORRIBLE

POSTIVE SELF-CARE AFFIRMATIONS:

1. IT'S OK TO BE OK
2. I AM SO WORTH THE EFFORT
3. I NEED TO LOVE AND RESPECT MYSELF
4. I AM ALLOWED TO PUT ME FIRST
5. I AM ALLOWED TO ASK FOR HELP
6. SELF-CARE IS A NECESSITY
7. I AM ALLOWED TO MESS UP
8. I AM DOING GOOD
9. I DESERVE TO BE HEALTHY AND SAFE
10. I AM ALLOWED SELF-CARE

1CORINTHIANS 10:31
"WHETHER THEREFORE YE EAT, OR DRINK, OR WHATSOEVER
YE DO, DO ALL TO THE GLORY OF GOD."

PONDER THE MOMENT
"LUKE 2:19"

PONDER THE MOMENT
"LUKE 2:19"

PONDER THE MOMENT
"LUKE 2:19"

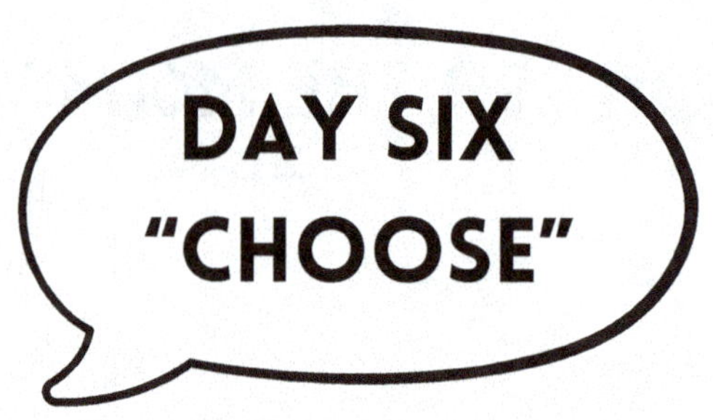

I WOKE UP FEELING

 AWESOME  GOOD  OKAY  NOT GOOD  HORRIBLE

REMEMBER WHEN CHOOSING WHAT IS BEST FOR YOU, IT MAY REQUIRE HELP FROM SOMEONE WHO WANTS TO SEE YOU GET BETTER.

FOOD FOR THOUGHT!!
YOU STILL HAVE THE FINAL SAY IN YOUR LIFE,
AND YOU CAN CHOOSE WHATEVER
IS BEST FOR YOU AS YOU NAVIGATE THROUGH THIS JOURNEY.
MAKE CHOICES ABOUT WHAT YOU CAN OR CAN'T DO, OR EVENTS YOU CAN ATTEND. DECIDING WHAT IS BEST FOR YOU HELPS YOU TO REINSTATE SOME CONTROL OVER YOUR LIFE.
GRIEF IS A STRANGE COMPLICATED THING. NO ONE CAN DICTATE HOW YOU GET THROUGH IT

"MAKE PLANS WITH YOUR NEEDS IN MIND
AND NOT THOSE OF OTHERS !!!"

WHAT CAN YOU DO TO CHOOSE YOU?

"REVELATION 21:4
AND GOD SHALL WIPE AWAY ALL TEARS FROM THEIR EYES;
AND THERE SHALL BE NO MORE DEATH, NEITHER SORROW, NOR CRYING,
NEITHER SHALL THERE BE ANY MORE PAIN: FOR THE FORMER
THINGS ARE PASSED AWAY."

PONDER THE MOMENT

"LUKE 2:19"

PONDER THE MOMENT

"LUKE 2:19"

PONDER THE MOMENT
"LUKE 2:19"

I WOKE UP FEELING

 AWESOME  GOOD  OKAY  NOT GOOD  HORRIBLE

GOD DESIGNED US FOR CONNECTION WITH OTHERS.
WHILE YOU ARE HURTING OR
GRIEVING DON'T LOSE YOUR CONNECTION IN LIFE.

"FOOD FOR THOUGHT "

ALTHOUGH NO ONE CAN FIX YOUR GRIEF BUT JESUS CHRIST. JUST HAVING ANOTHER PERSON PRESENT BY YOUR SIDE WITHOUT JUDGEMENT OR SAYING A WORD CAN HELP IMMENSELY. YOU ARE NOT MEANT TO DO THIS ALONE. IT'S DIFFICULT BUT IMPORTANT NOT TO REMOVE YOURSELF FROM EVERYONE, EVEN THOUGH THAT IS THE EASY WAY OUT. IT'S ALSO IMPORTANT NOT TO MASK YOUR FEELINGS. WHEN ASKED JUST BE HONEST, THAT IS WHAT PEOPLE NEED TO HEAR. UNDERSTAND THIS, THEY CAN'T HELP YOU IF YOU ARE NOT BEING HONEST.

WHO IS THE ONE PERSON YOU CAN REACH OUT TO NO MATTER WHAT?

PROVERBS 18:24
"A MAN THAT HATH FRIENDS MUST SHEW HIMSELF FRIENDLY:
AND THERE IS A FRIEND THAT STICKETH CLOSER THAN A BROTHER."

PONDER THE MOMENT
"LUKE 2:19"

PONDER THE MOMENT
"LUKE 2:19"

PONDER THE MOMENT
"LUKE 2:19"

I WOKE UP FEELING

 AWESOME  GOOD  OKAY  NOT GOOD  HORRIBLE

DEFINE COMMUNICATE:

____

____

"FOOD FOR THOUGHT"
GRIEF IS HARD!!! JUST BECAUSE YOU ARE GRIEVING DOESN'T MEAN YOU ARE A BURDEN TO THOSE AROUND YOU.
WE NEED TO COMMUNICATE OUR FEELING.
IF YOU DON'T TALK, NO ONE WILL KNOW HOW TO HELP YOU. PUT YOUR NEEDS OUT THERE.
BE HONEST WITH YOURSELF AND OTHERS.
" A CLOSED MOUTH DOESN'T GET FED"

IT'S OKAY TO NOT BE OKAY!!!!

NAME ONE THING THAT YOU CAN COMMUNICATE BETTER?

____

____

PSALM 73:24,26
"THOU SHALT GUIDE ME WITH THY COUNSEL, AND AFTERWARD RECEIVE ME TO GLORY. MY FLESH AND MY HEART FAILETH: BUT GOD IS THE STRENGTH OF MY HEART, AND MY PORTION FOR EVER."

PONDER THE MOMENT
"LUKE 2:19"

PONDER THE MOMENT
"LUKE 2:19"

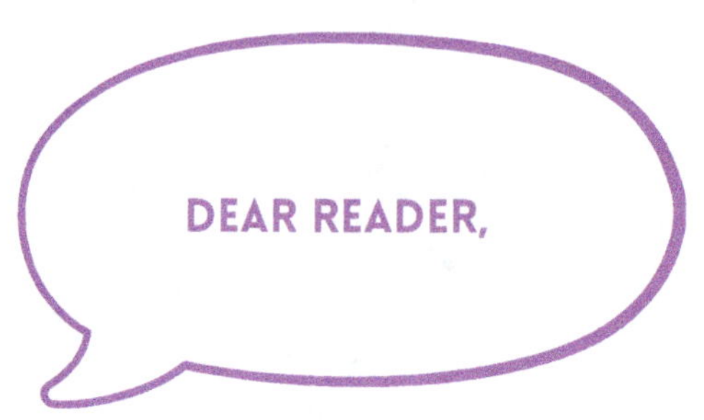

THROUGHOUT THE CREATION OF THIS BOOK, I DISCOVERED
HOW POWERFUL STORYTELLING IS WHEN DEALING WITH
LOSS. EACH WORD WRITTEN GAVE ME HOPE AND HEALING;
NOW, I WISH TO
SHARE THESE WORDS WITH OTHERS GOING THROUGH SIMILAR
EXPERIENCES WILL KNOW THEY AREN'T ALONE.

YOURS TRULY,
LAWANDA WALKER-TAVE

PONDER THE MOMENT
"LUKE 2:19"

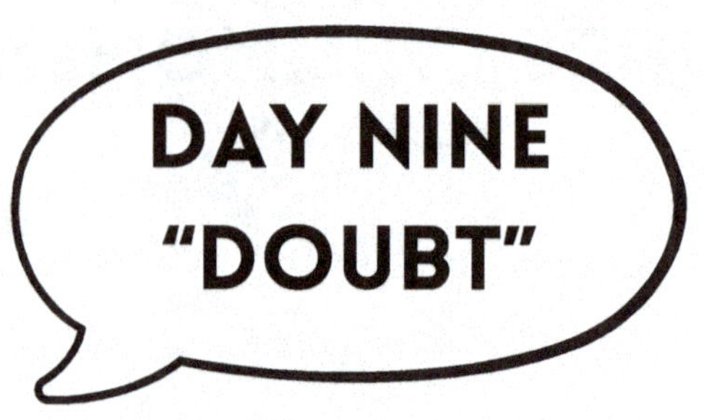

I WOKE UP FEELING

AWESOME   **GOOD**   **OKAY**   **NOT GOOD**   **HORRIBLE**

MEMORIZE THE DEFINITION OF DOUBT:
DOUBT-IS AN ATTITUDE OF UNBELIEF, CHARACTER
MIXED BY REBELLION AND DISOBEDIENCE TOWARDS GOD

HOW IS DOUBT AFFECTING YOU?

____

____

TRUST GOD EVEN IN THE HARD TIMES. EVEN WHEN GRIEF SEEMS TO
BE A CONSTANT COMPANION, TRUSTING GOD IS VERY POSSIBLE.
IN YOUR TIME OF GRIEF, CHOOSE TO TRUST GOD. HE HASN'T
LEFT YOU AND HAS A PERFECT PLAN FOR YOUR LIFE AFTER GRIEF.

WHEN WE FAIL TO EXERCISE PROPER FAITH, WE REPLACE IT
WITH A LOT OF DOUBT.YOU EITHER BELIEVE GOD
CAN HELP YOU WITH YOUR GRIEF OR NOT.
WILL YOU ALLOW GOD TO HELP YOU.

WHAT ARE YOU DOUBTING THAT YOU THINK GOD CAN'T FIX OR
HEAL?

JAMES 1:5,
"IF ANY OF YOU LACK WISDOM, LET HIM ASK OF GOD,
THAT GIVETH TO ALL MEN LIBERALLY, AND UPBRAIDETH NOT;
AND IT SHALL BE GIVEN HIM. "

PONDER THE MOMENT
"LUKE 2:19"

PONDER THE MOMENT
"LUKE 2:19"

PONDER THE MOMENT
"LUKE 2:19"

I WOKE UP FEELING

AWESOME **GOOD** **OKAY** **NOT GOOD** **HORRIBLE**

"6 WAYS TO IMPROVE YOUR MENTAL HEALTH"

1. TRY TO RELAX AND REDUCE STRESS.
2. FIND WAYS TO LEARN A NEW HOBBY.
3. SPEND TIME IN NATURE.
4. LOOK AFTER YOUR PHYSICAL HEALTH.
5. WORK ON IMPROVING YOUR SLEEP.
6. EAT HEALTHIER

WHICH ONE CAN YOU WORK ON TODAY?

SELF-CARE BOUNDARIES

I WILL NOT PUT MYSELF LAST..........
I WILL NOT ALLOW DRAMA..............
I WILL NOT BE DISRESPECTED..........
I WILL NOT BE MANIPULATED........
I WILL NOT NEGLECT MY HEALTH.....
I WILL NOT COMPARE MYSELF TO OTHERS......

REVELATION 21:4
"AND GOD SHALL WIPE AWAY ALL TEARS FROM THEIR EYES;
AND THERE SHALL BE NO MORE DEATH,
NEITHER SORROW, NOR CRYING, NEITHER SHALL THERE BE ANY MORE PAIN:
FOR THE FORMER THINGS ARE PASSED AWAY."

PONDER THE MOMENT
"LUKE 2:19"

PONDER THE MOMENT
"LUKE 2:19"

PONDER THE MOMENT
"LUKE 2:19"

I WOKE UP FEELING

 AWESOME
 GOOD
 OKAY
 NOT GOOD
 HORRIBLE

TODAY WE REMEMBER OUR LOVED ONE!!

PLACE A PICTURE
OF YOUR LOVED ONE
HERE

WHAT IS ONE THING YOU MISS ABOUT THEM?

____

____

WHAT IS SOMETHING THEY WOULD ALWAYS SAY?

____

____

IF YOU COULD TELL THEM ANYTHING WHAT WOULD IT BE?

____

____

1 JOHN 4:8
"HE THAT LOVETH NOT KNOWETH NOT GOD; FOR GOD IS LOVE."

PONDER THE MOMENT
"LUKE 2:19"

PONDER THE MOMENT
"LUKE 2:19"

PONDER THE MOMENT
"LUKE 2:19"

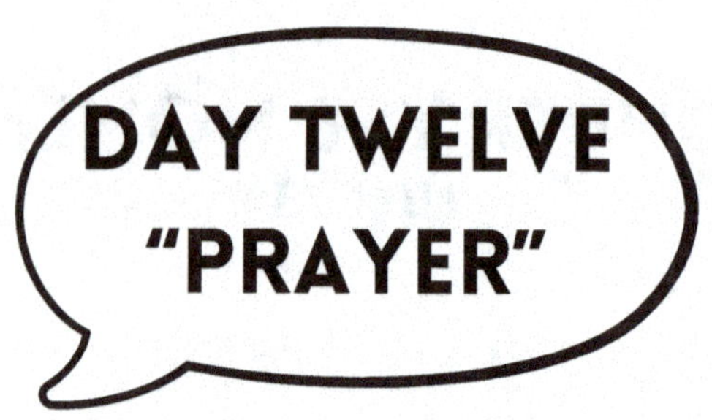

I WOKE UP FEELING

 AWESOME
 GOOD
 OKAY
 NOT GOOD
 HORRIBLE

-PRAYER-
THE ACT OF ASKING GOD TO DO WHAT
HE HAS ALREADY PROMISED TO DO.
BASICALLY IT IS COMMUNICATION WITH GOD.

PRAYER IS ONE OF THE MOST POWERFUL WAYS TO
DEAL WITH GRIEF BECAUSE,
YOU ARE TALKING TO THE ONLY ONE THAT CAN TRULY HEAL YOU.
PRAYER LETS ONE EXPRESS THEIR FEELINGS IN A PRIVATE YET
PERSONAL WAY. GOD UNDERSTANDS US WHEN IT COMES
TO GRIEVING, BECAUSE HE ALSO LOST HIS ONLY SON.

WHAT DOES PRAYER MEAN TO YOU?

"IF YOU DON'T FEEL LIKE PRAYING, FORCE IT BECAUSE SOMETHING
IS FORCING YOU NOT TO PRAY"

HOW HAS PRAYER HELPED YOU DURING YOUR GRIEF JOURNEY?

JOHN 14:14
"IF YE SHALL ASK ANY THING IN MY NAME, I WILL DO IT."

PONDER THE MOMENT
"LUKE 2:19"

PONDER THE MOMENT
"LUKE 2:19"

PONDER THE MOMENT
"LUKE 2:19"

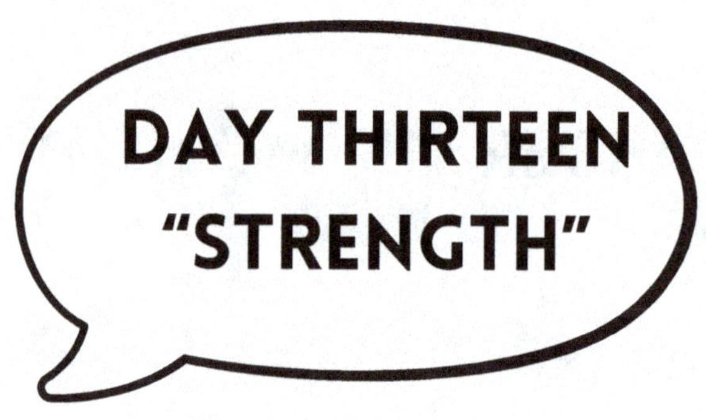

I WOKE UP FEELING

 AWESOME  GOOD  OKAY  NOT GOOD  HORRIBLE

STRENGTH

THE CAPACITY OF AN OBJECT OR SUBSTANCE TO WITHSTAND GREAT FORCE OR PRESSURE

GOD GIVES STRENGTH TO THE WEARY AND INCREASES THE POWER OF THE WEAK. THERE HAVE BEEN TIMES WHERE I COULDN'T FIND THE STRENGTH TO GET OUT OF BED. THE ONE PERSON I KNEW THAT COULD GIVE ME STRENGTH IS THE ONE I CALLED ON WHICH IS GOD. IT'S OK IF WE DON'T HAVE THE STRENGTH TO FIGHT BECAUSE WE HAVE A SAVIOR WHO IS READY AND WILLING TO FIGHT FOR US ONE MORE DAY.

WHO DO YOU DRAW YOUR STRENGTH FROM?

____

____

HOW HAS YOUR STRENGTH HELPED YOU WITH YOUR GRIEF?

____

____

____

PSALM 46:1
"GOD IS OUR REFUGE AND STRENGTH, A VERY PRESENT HELP IN TROUBLE."

PONDER THE MOMENT
"LUKE 2:19"

PONDER THE MOMENT
"LUKE 2:19"

PONDER THE MOMENT
"LUKE 2:19"

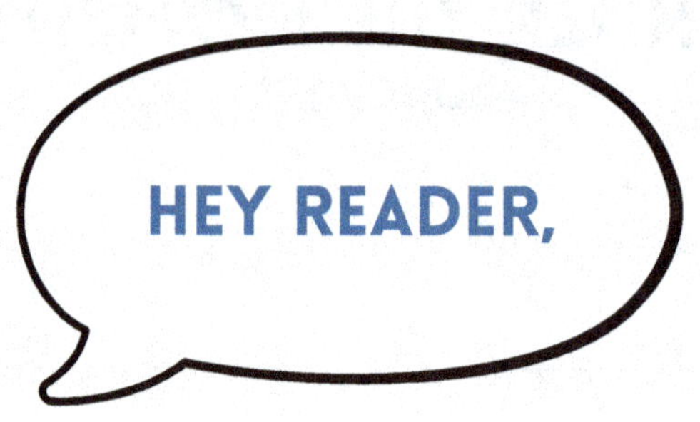

IN CASE YOU HAVEN'T NOTICED, LIFE ISN'T ALWAYS EASY.
AND WHEN WE'RE SMACK IN THE MIDDLE OF HEARTACHE,
FORWARD MOTION SEEMS ABOUT AS LIKELY AS SPOTTING
BIGFOOT RIDING A UNICORN.
BUT FEAR NOT, MY FRIEND BECAUSE YOURS TRULY FOUND
AN AWESOME
COPING MECHANISM - WRITING THIS BOOK!
IT WAS CHOCK-FULL OF 'AHA MOMENTS', MAKING OUR
PROTAGONIST (YOURS TRULY) FEEL ALL SORTS OF
EMPOWERED WHILE STROLLING THROUGH THE VALLEY OF
TEARS. SO YEAH, GRIEF IS LAME,
BUT IT CANNOT CONSUME US ENTIRELY. WE GOT THIS!!!

YOURS TRULY,
LAWANDA WALKER-TAVE

PONDER THE MOMENT
"LUKE 2:19"

PONDER THE MOMENT
"LUKE 2:19"

PONDER THE MOMENT
"LUKE 2:19"

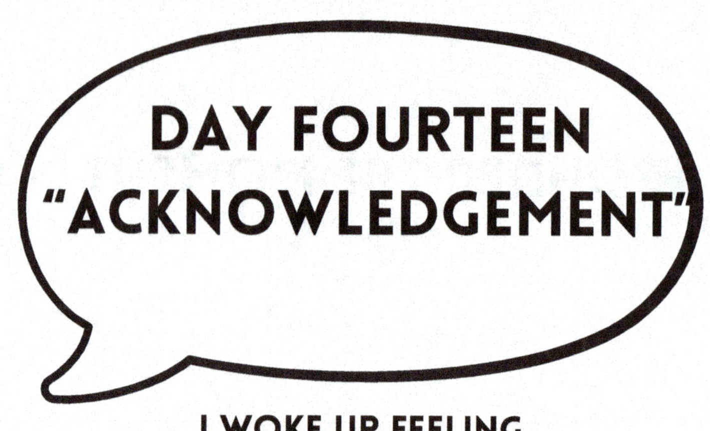

I WOKE UP FEELING

AWESOME   GOOD   OKAY   NOT GOOD   HORRIBLE

ACKNOWLEDGEMENT –ACCEPTING OF THE TRUTH OR EXERCISE OF SOMETHING SELF-AWARENESS, ACCEPTANCE

"A FEW THINGS TO HELP YOU ACKNOWLEDGE YOUR GRIEF"
RECOGNIZE THE MANY COLORS OF GRIEF...
PREPARE YOURSELF FOR THE NEXT STEP....
SCHEDULE A TIME TO GRIEVE IF YOU NEED TO...

**WHAT ARE 6 OF THE HARDEST THINGS
THAT YOU HAVE HAD TO ACKNOWLEDGE IN THIS GRIEF JOURNEY?**

1.   4.
2.   5.
3.   6.

COMING TO TERMS WITH MY SON'S PASSING REMAINS ONE OF LIFE'S GREATEST CHALLENGES FOR ME – KNOWING HE WILL NEVER AGAIN BE PHYSICALLY PRESENT NOR AUDIBLE. THROUGH THIS STRUGGLE THOUGH, THE TEMPORAL NATURE OF HUMANITY'S TIME ON EARTH BECAME CLEAR-CUT TRUTH IN MY EYES. MORTALITY ULTIMATELY USHERS EACH PERSON INTO THEIR NEXT JOURNEY.

PONDER THE MOMENT
"LUKE 2:19"

PONDER THE MOMENT
"LUKE 2:19"

PONDER THE MOMENT
"LUKE 2:19"

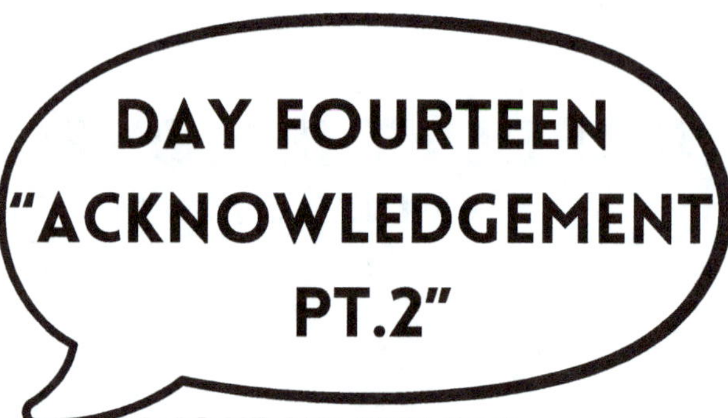

I WOKE UP FEELING

| AWESOME | GOOD | OKAY | NOT GOOD | HORRIBLE |

"SIX STEPS TO ATTENDING TO YOUR GRIEF"

•ACKNOWLEDGING THE REALITY OF DEATH.

•REMEMBERING THE PERSON WHO DIED.

• EMBRACING THE PAIN OF LOSS

•FINDING SUPPORT IN FRIEND, FAMILY, OR A THERAPIST

•FINDING THE MEANING OF DEATH. (IT'S OK TO ASK QUESTIONS)

•FIGURING OUT THE NEW YOU.

WHAT EMOTION HAVE YOU HAD TO ACKNOWLEDGE THE MOST ON THIS JOURNEY?

____

____

____

____

(SO DON'T BURY YOUR FEELINGS)

PROVERBS 3:5,
"TRUST IN THE LORD WITH ALL THINE HEART; AND LEAN
NOT UNTO THINE OWN UNDERSTANDING."

PONDER THE MOMENT
"LUKE 2:19"

PONDER THE MOMENT
"LUKE 2:19"

PONDER THE MOMENT
"LUKE 2:19"

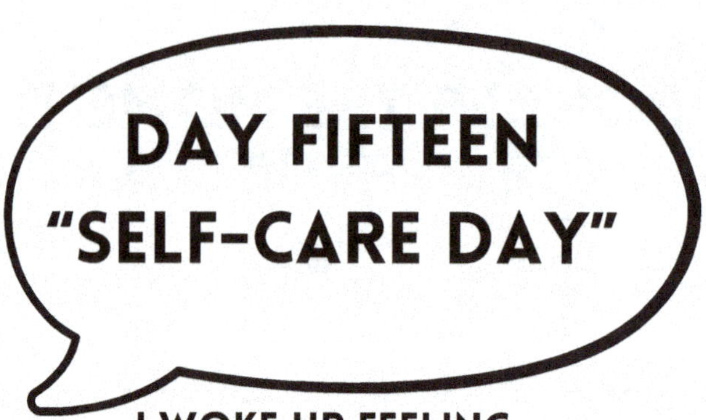

I WOKE UP FEELING

AWESOME   GOOD   OKAY   NOT GOOD   HORRIBLE

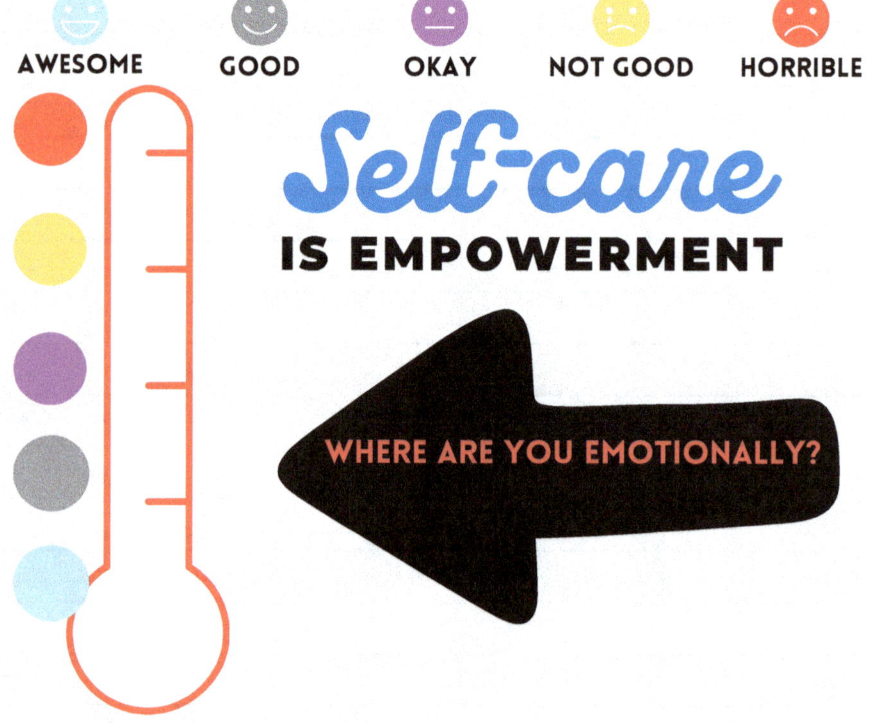

WHAT EMOTION ARE YOU FEELING TODAY AND WHY ?

____
____
____
____

1 JOHN 4:19
WE LOVE HIM, BECAUSE HE FIRST LOVED US."

PONDER THE MOMENT
"LUKE 2:19"

PONDER THE MOMENT
"LUKE 2:19"

PONDER THE MOMENT
"LUKE 2:19"

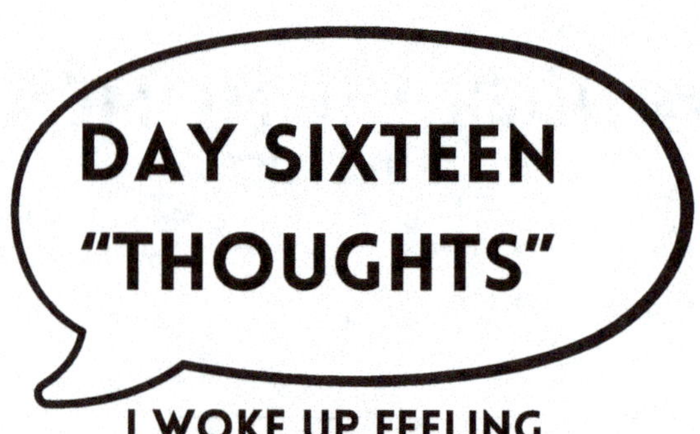

I WOKE UP FEELING

 **AWESOME**　 **GOOD**　 **OKAY**　 **NOT GOOD**　 **HORRIBLE**

PONDER THE MOMENT
*WHAT IS ON YOUR HEART TODAY?"

LUKE 2:19
"BUT MARY KEPT ALL THESE THINGS, AND PONDERED THEM IN HER HEART."

PONDER THE MOMENT
"LUKE 2:19"

PONDER THE MOMENT
"LUKE 2:19"

PONDER THE MOMENT
"LUKE 2:19"

I WOKE UP FEELING

AWESOME   GOOD   OKAY   NOT GOOD   HORRIBLE

-BIBLICAL HOPE-
TO BELIEVE THAT WHAT IS DESIRED CAN BE
HAD OR WILL TURN OUT FOR THE BEST.

"RELYING ON YOUR FAITH DURING HARD TIMES"
1. MAINTAIN YOUR FAITH AT ALL TIMES...
2. DON'T SEPARATE THE GOOD TIMES OR HARD TIMES FROM YOUR FAITH...
3. FIND WAYS THAT BRING YOU PEACE. ...
4. LAY YOUR TRIALS AND HEARTACHES BEFORE GOD...
5. RELY ON YOUR SUPPORT SYSTEM...

LET US NOT BE SURPRISED WHEN WE HAVE TO FACE DIFFICULTIES.
WHEN THE WIND BLOWS HARD ON A TREE, THE ROOTS STRETCH
AND GROW STRONGER. LET IT BE THIS WAY WITH US.
LET US NOT BE WEAKLINGS, YIELDING TO EVERY WIND
THAT BLOWS, BUT STRONG IN SPIRIT TO RESIST.

WHAT 3 THINGS WOULD YOU LIKE TO LEARN DURING THIS TIME?
1.
2.
3.

ROMANS 8:39
"NOR HEIGHT, NOR DEPTH, NOR ANY OTHER CREATURE, SHALL BE ABLE
TO SEPARATE US FROM THE LOVE OF GOD, WHICH IS IN
CHRIST JESUS OUR LORD."

PONDER THE MOMENT
"LUKE 2:19"

PONDER THE MOMENT
"LUKE 2:19"

PONDER THE MOMENT
"LUKE 2:19"

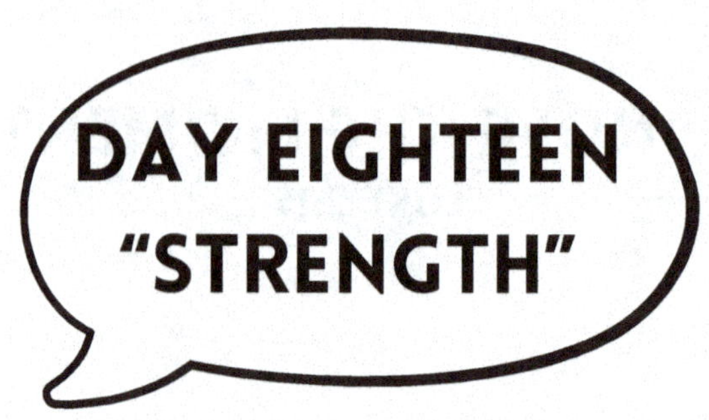

I WOKE UP FEELING

 AWESOME  GOOD  OKAY  NOT GOOD  HORRIBLE

STRENGTH- THE QUALITY OR STATE OF BEING PHYSICALLY STRONG.

BIBLICAL STRENGTH- THE ENERGY OF GOD A PLACE OR MEANS OF SAFETY, PROTECTION, OR STRONGHOLD.

DEFINE STRENGTH IN YOUR OWN WORDS?

HOW TO WALK IN GOD'S STRENGTH:

1. GET SAVED OR BORN AGAIN .
2. LEARN TO WAIT ON GOD.
3. TRUST GOD AND MAKE HIM YOUR ONLY STRENGTH
4. MAINTAIN A LIFE OF PRAISE AND WORSHIP.
5. CONSISTENT PRAYER

PICK 3 POWER WORDS TO HELP YOU IN THE NEXT 7 DAYS.
1.
2.
3.

PSALM 126:5
THEY THAT SOW IN TEARS SHALL REAP IN JOY."

PONDER THE MOMENT
"LUKE 2:19"

PONDER THE MOMENT
"LUKE 2:19"

PONDER THE MOMENT
"LUKE 2:19"

I WOKE UP FEELING

AWESOME	GOOD	OKAY	NOT GOOD	HORRIBLE

TRUST
1.) A FIRM BELIEF IN LIABILITY OR STRENGTH OF SOMEONE OR SOMETHING.
2.) TO PUT YOUR COMPLETE TRUST IN THE LORD.

VERSES ON TRUST

JOHN 17:17
NUMBERS 23:19
PROVERBS 28:26
PSALM 62:8
PSALM 118:8
PSALM 40:3

A BIBLICAL EXAMPLE OF TRUST?
MATTHEW 14:22-33,
PETER HAD SO MUCH TRUST IN JESUS THAT HE WAS ABLE TO WALK ON WATER,
UNTIL HE TOOK HIS EYES OFF JESUS, AND JESUS WAS RIGHT IN FRONT OF HIM.

WHAT DOES TRUST MEAN SPIRITUALLY?
TO PLACE YOUR CONFIDENCE ONLY IN GOD AND NOT MAN.
WHY IS TRUST SO IMPORTANT TO GOD?
HAVING FAITH IS HAVING TRUST.

PONDER THE MOMENT

"LUKE 2:19"

PONDER THE MOMENT
"LUKE 2:19"

PONDER THE MOMENT
"LUKE 2:19"

HOW CAN YOU TRUST GOD MORE?

GOD KNOWS WHAT IS BEST FOR YOU. YOU HAVE TO TRULY EMBRACE AND
TRUST WHAT HE HAS PLANNED FOR YOU,
EVEN IF IT INCLUDES BREAKING YOUR HEART BY LOSING A LOVED ONE.
OUR TRUST IS NOT FOOLISH OR SILLY.
(DON'T LET ANYONE TELL YOU DIFFERENTLY)
FOR OUR GOD IS BOTH FAITHFUL AND GOOD.

HOW CAN WE TRUST GOD AND STILL BE FAITHFUL
DURING DIFFICULT TIMES?
DON'T LET YOUR EMOTIONS RULE YOUR LIFE.
WE NEED TO BRING THEM TO GOD SO THAT
HE CAN HELP US TO ADDRESS THEM FROM HIS POINT OF VIEW.
1.START YOUR DAY BY GIVING IT TO GOD
2.PLEASE DON'T TAKE YESTERDAY'S MISTAKES
INTO THE CLEAN SLATE OF TODAY
3.OPEN YOUR BIBLE AND LISTEN TO GOD

MICAH 7:5
"TRUST YE NOT IN A FRIEND, PUT YE NOT CONFIDENCE IN A GUIDE:
KEEP THE DOORS OF THY MOUTH FROM HER
THAT LIETH IN THY BOSOM."

PONDER THE MOMENT
"LUKE 2:19"

PONDER THE MOMENT
"LUKE 2:19"

PONDER THE MOMENT
"LUKE 2:19"

I WOKE UP FEELING

"YOUR ANXIETY IS WORTH MANAGING "
THIS WORRY JAR IS AN EFFECTIVE TOOL THAT WILL HELP YOU TO EXPRESS YOUR ANXIOUS THOUGHTS AND WORRIES. TAKE A MOMENT AND THINK ABOUT WHAT MAKES YOU ANXIOUS. JOT IT DOWN ON A PIECE OF PAPER AND PLACE IN YOUR WORRY JAR.

YOUR WORRY JAR!

FOR THIS ACTIVITY YOU WILL NEED AN ACTUAL JAR!

THINK OF A SPECIFIC TIME EACH DAY WHEN YOU WILL OPEN YOUR WORRY JAR AND READ YOUR WORRIES. THIS CAN BE DONE WITH SOMEONE YOU TRUST OR NOT. AFTER YOU ARE DONE READING THEM GIVE THEM TO GOD.

WHAT TIME WILL YOU OPEN YOUR WORRY JAR?

WHO WILL BE WITH YOU?

PSALMS 5:1
"GIVE EAR TO MY WORDS, O LORD, CONSIDER MY MEDITATION."

PONDER THE MOMENT

"LUKE 2:19"

PONDER THE MOMENT
"LUKE 2:19"

PONDER THE MOMENT
"LUKE 2:19"

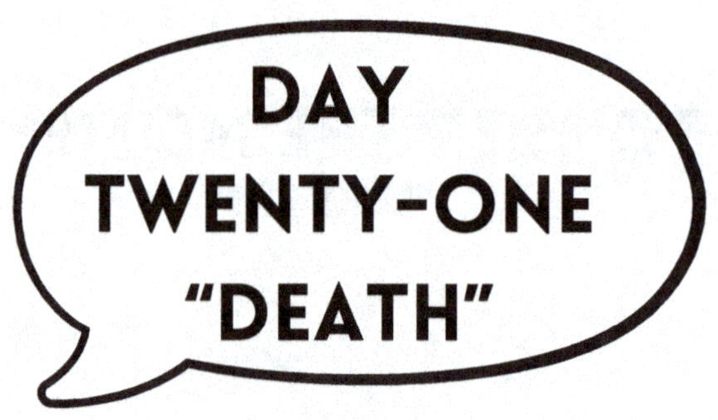

I WOKE UP FEELING

AWESOME	GOOD	OKAY	NOT GOOD	HORRIBLE

DEATH- THE ACTION OR FACT OF DYING OR BEING KILLED; THE END OF THE LIFE OF A PERSON OR ORGANISM

DEFINE DEATH IN YOUR OWN WORDS-

"HOW TO ACCEPT THE DEATH OF A LOVED ONE"
1. ACCEPT YOUR FEELINGS
2. TALK ABOUT THE DEATH OF YOUR LOVED ONE
3. REACH OUT AND HELP OTHERS WHO ARE GRIEVING

THERE ARE 5 ATTITUDES TOWARDS DEATH
1. DEATH ANXIETY
2. DEATH FEAR
3. DEATH AVOIDANCE
4. POSITIVE ATTITUDE
5. ESCAPE ACCEPTANCE

WHAT IS YOUR ATTITUDE TOWARDS DEATH?

PONDER THE MOMENT
"LUKE 2:19"

PONDER THE MOMENT
"LUKE 2:19"

PONDER THE MOMENT
"LUKE 2:19"

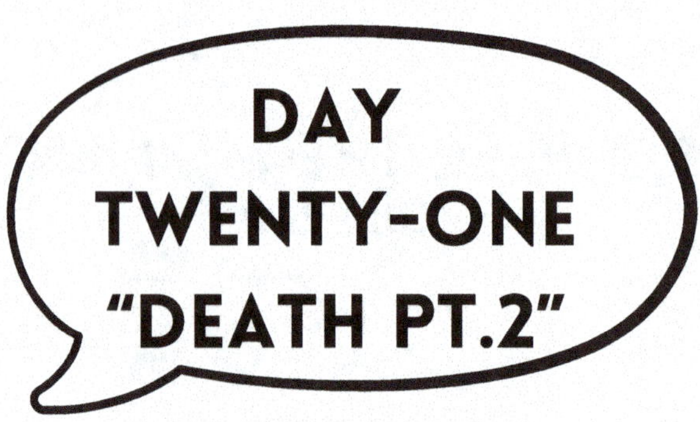

I WOKE UP FEELING

AWESOME   GOOD   OKAY   NOT GOOD   HORRIBLE

THERE ARE 5 TYPES OF DEATH
1.NATURAL
2.ACCIDENT
3.SUICIDE
4.HOMICIDE
5.UNDETERMINED/PENDING

HOW TO ACCEPT DEATH AND NOT FEAR IT ANYMORE...
1.ACCEPT DEATH
2.LET THE KNOWLEDGE OF DEATH HELP YOU APPRECIATE LIFE
3. FIND THE SUPPORT YOU NEED FOR WHATEVER YOU NEED
HELP WITH

"REMEMBER DEATH AND GRIEF AFFECTS EVERYONE DIFFERENTLY.
YOUR GRIEF IS YOUR OWN!!"

WHAT DOES THE BIBLE SAY ABOUT DEATH?
1.DEATH IS INEVITABLE (EVERYONE WILL EXPERIENCE IT)
2.IT'S A SEPARATION (JAMES 2:26)
3.DEATH WILL DIE AND OUR SOUL WILL LIVE ON (REV.20:14)

ECCLESIASTES 3:2
"A TIME TO BE BORN, AND A TIME TO DIE; A TIME TO PLANT,
AND A TIME TO PLUCK UP THAT WHICH IS PLANTED;"

PONDER THE MOMENT
"LUKE 2:19"

PONDER THE MOMENT

"LUKE 2:19"

PONDER THE MOMENT
"LUKE 2:19"

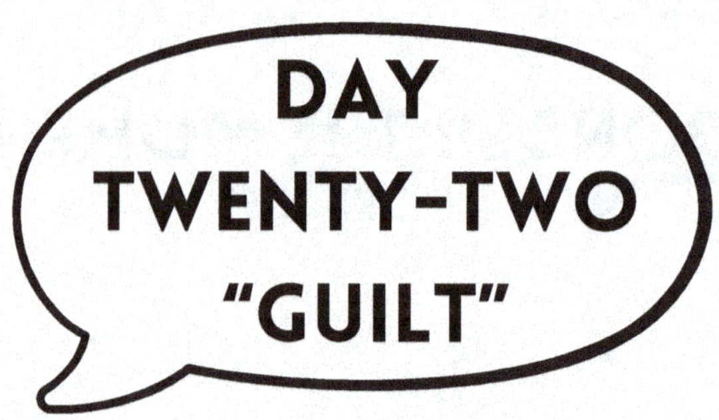

I WOKE UP FEELING

| AWESOME | GOOD | OKAY | NOT GOOD | HORRIBLE |

WHAT IS SURVIVOR'S GUILT-
A MENTAL CONDITION THAT OCCURS WHEN A PERSON BELIEVES THEY HAVE DONE SOMETHING WRONG BY SURVIVING A TRAUMATIC OR TRAGIC EVENT WHEN OTHERS DON'T .

WHAT ARE YOUR THOUGHTS ON SURVIVOR'S GUILT?

"SIGNS THAT YOU ARE EXPERIENCING SURVIVOR'S GUILT"

1. SUICIDAL THOUGHTS
2. SOCIAL WITHDRAWAL
3. DIFFICULTY SLEEPING
4. PHYSICAL SYMPTOMS
(LIKE HEADACHES OR DIZZINESS)
5. FLASHBACKS OR NIGHTMARES
OF WHAT HAS HAPPENED

PONDER THE MOMENT
"LUKE 2:19"

PONDER THE MOMENT
"LUKE 2:19"

PONDER THE MOMENT
"LUKE 2:19"

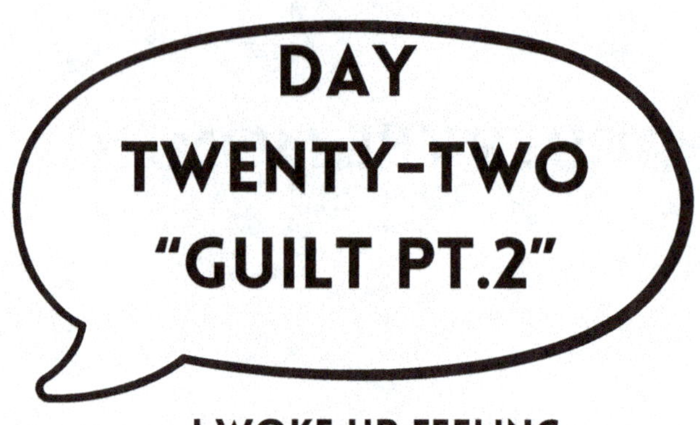

I WOKE UP FEELING

| AWESOME | GOOD | OKAY | NOT GOOD | HORRIBLE |

2 TYPES OF SURVIVOR'S GUILT

1. FEELING GUILTY ABOUT SURVIVING WHEN YOUR LOVE ONE DIED
2. THOSE WHO FEEL GUILTY THAT ANOTHER PERSON DIED BY SAVING YOUR LOVE ONE

WAYS TO HELP YOU COPE:

1. ALLOW YOURSELF TO GRIEVE
2. PRACTICE SELF-FORGIVENESS (EASIER SAID THAN DONE)
3. REMEMBER YOUR FEELINGS ARE COMMON AND THEY ARE ALSO NORMAL

WHAT ARE SOME WAYS THAT CAN HELP YOU CAN GET THROUGH SURVIVOR'S GUILT

1.

2.

3.

EPHESIANS 2:4
"BUT GOD, WHO IS RICH IN MERCY, FOR HIS GREAT LOVE WHEREWITH HE LOVED US,"

PONDER THE MOMENT
"LUKE 2:19"

PONDER THE MOMENT
"LUKE 2:19"

PONDER THE MOMENT
"LUKE 2:19"

I WOKE UP FEELING

 AWESOME
 GOOD
 OKAY
 NOT GOOD
 HORRIBLE

MEMORIZE THE DEFINITION OF HEALING.

HEALING- THE PROCESS OF MAKING OR BECOMING SOUND OR HEALTHY AGAIN.

KEY FACTS ABOUT HEALING

GRIEF IS NORMAL (IT'S NOT A DISEASE)

THE WORST KIND OF GRIEF IS YOUR OWN

THE WAY OUT OF GRIEF IS TO WALK THROUGH IT.

(GRIEF IS PAINFUL, AND THERE IS NO WAY AROUND IT)

GRIEF IS UNPREDICTABLE, IT COMES AND GOES AT ITS OWN PACE

WHAT IN YOUR LIFE NEEDS TO BE HEALED?

-A FEW THINGS YOU CAN DO TO START THE HEALING PROCESS-

>TAKE CARE OF YOURSELF

>MOST IMPORTANTLY ALLOW YOURSELF TO GRIEVE

(IT'S OK TO CRY, SCREAM, AND EVEN BE ANGRY)

GOD UNDERSTANDS OUR TEARS.

>ACCEPT YOUR EMOTIONS FOR WHAT THEY ARE.

>ACKNOWLEDGE YOUR PAIN

>EMBRACE YOUR GRIEF

PONDER THE MOMENT
"LUKE 2:19"

PONDER THE MOMENT
"LUKE 2:19"

PONDER THE MOMENT
"LUKE 2:19"

I WOKE UP FEELING

 AWESOME  GOOD  OKAY  NOT GOOD  HORRIBLE

"HOW DOES GOD WANT US TO HEAL"

OUR HEAVENLY FATHER KNOWS WE WILL EXPERIENCE GRIEF IN OUR LIFETIME ,WE ARE NOT MEANT TO GO THROUGH THIS ALONE. !!EVEN WHEN IT HURTS AND IT WILL HURT (PRAISE GOD ANYWAY)!! ONE THING I WILL SAY IS LET GOD WALK YOU THROUGH YOUR GRIEF JOURNEY. SOME OF US(INCLUDING ME AT ONE POINT) SORROWED AS IF WE DON'T HAVE THE HOPE OF SEEING OUR LOVED ONES AGAIN. THAT'S NOT HOW GOD DESIGNED THIS JOURNEY. HE WANTS US TO SORROW WITH HOPE. WE MUST OPERATE ACCORDING TO HEAVEN'S RULES NOT OURS. DON'T ALLOW YOUR SORROW TO DRIVE YOU AWAY FROM GOD, CHURCH YOUR FRIENDS, OR FAMILY.

LET GOD HEAL   YOUR BROKEN HEART.

WHAT CAN YOU DO TO START YOU HEALING JOURNEY THROUGH YOUR GRIEF?

HOSEA 6:1

"COME, AND LET US RETURN UNTO THE LORD: FOR HE HATH TORN, AND HE WILL HEAL US; HE HATH SMITTEN, AND HE WILL BIND US UP."

PONDER THE MOMENT
"LUKE 2:19"

PONDER THE MOMENT
"LUKE 2:19"

PONDER THE MOMENT
"LUKE 2:19"

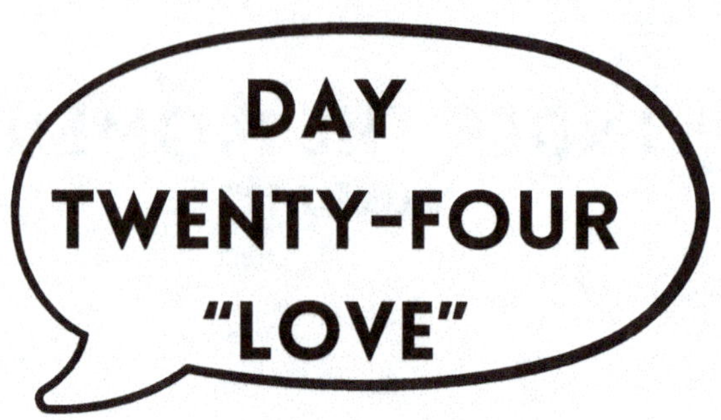

I WOKE UP FEELING

AWESOME　　GOOD　　OKAY　　NOT GOOD　　HORRIBLE

LOVE- AN INTENSE FEELING OF DEEP AFFECTION

4 TYPES OF LOVE

(WHICH LOVE REPRESENTS YOU):

***PHILIA- FRIENDSHIP**
***EROS-SENSUAL/ROMANTIC LOVE**
***STORGE-LOVE OF FAMILY**
***AGAPA-PERFECT/UNCONDITIONAL LOVE**

WHEN WE LOVE HARD, WE GRIEVE HARDER BUT JESUS LOVES DEEPER. GRIEF IS LOVE WITH NO WHERE TO GO. WHERE DO WE PUT ALL THIS LOVE WE HAVE LEFT? YOU COULD INVEST THAT LOVE INTO SOMEONE ELSE WHO IS STARTING OUT ON THEIR OWN GRIEF JOURNEY YOU COULD ALSO LOVE ON YOUR FAMILY MORE.

WHO CAN YOU INVEST YOUR LOVE INTO AND WHY?

PONDER THE MOMENT
"LUKE 2:19"

PONDER THE MOMENT
"LUKE 2:19"

PONDER THE MOMENT
"LUKE 2:19"

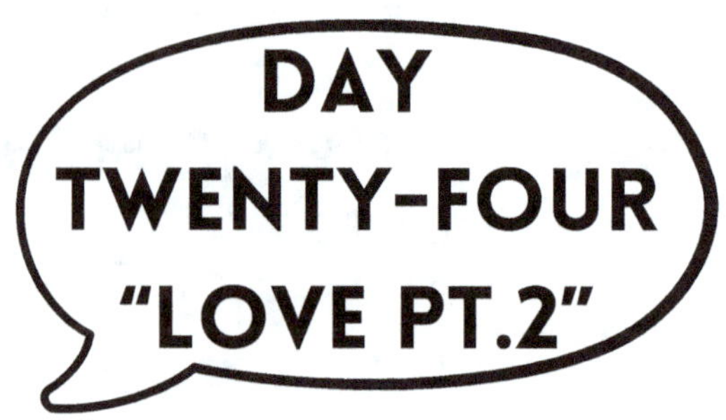

I WOKE UP FEELING

 AWESOME  GOOD  OKAY  NOT GOOD  HORRIBLE

LOVE-

GRIEF IS OUR PRICELESS GIFT OF LOVE. WHEN THERE IS DEEP GRIEF,
THERE IS GREAT LOVE. IF YOU ALLOW YOURSELF TO LOVE, YOU MUST
ALSO ALLOW YOURSELF TO GRIEVE.

DO YOU HAVE A FAVORITE VERSE ON LOVE?

____

____

BIBLE VERSE ON LOVE

DUETERONOMY 7:9 -GOD'S FAITHFULNESS
AND LOVE
LEVITICUS 19:18- LOVE FOR OUR ENEMIES
SONG OF SOLOMON 8:6,7- LOVE BETWEEN
HUSBAND AND WIFE

1JOHN 4:11
"BELOVED, IF GOD SO LOVED US, WE OUGHT ALSO TO LOVE ONE ANOTHER."

PONDER THE MOMENT
"LUKE 2:19"

PONDER THE MOMENT
"LUKE 2:19"

PONDER THE MOMENT
"LUKE 2:19"

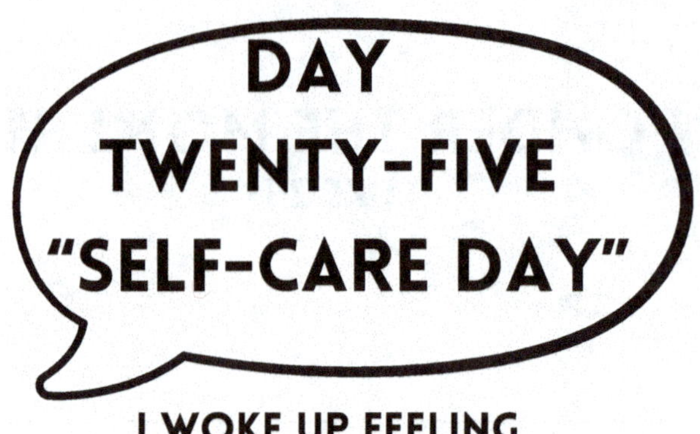

I WOKE UP FEELING

AWESOME   GOOD   OKAY   NOT GOOD   HORRIBLE

"WRITE A LETTER TO YOURSELF "

Q DEAR ME,   ✕

LOVE, MYSELF

1 THESSALONIANS 5:17
"PRAY WITHOUT CEASING."

PONDER THE MOMENT
"LUKE 2:19"

PONDER THE MOMENT
"LUKE 2:19"

PONDER THE MOMENT
"LUKE 2:19"

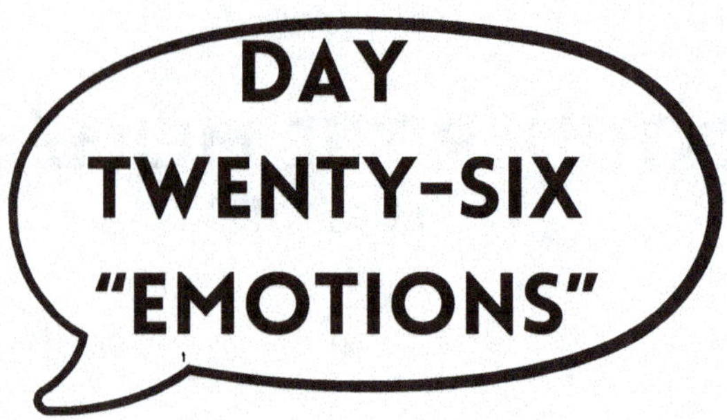

I WOKE UP FEELING

AWESOME   GOOD   OKAY   NOT GOOD   HORRIBLE

EMOTIONS-
A NATURAL INSTINCTIVE
STATE OF MIND DERIVING FROM ONE'S
CIRCUMSTANCE, MOOD,
OR RELATIONSHIP WITH OTHER.

8 TYPES OF EMOTIONS....

- HAPPINESS
- SADNESS
- DISGUST
- DEPRESSION
- STRESS
- ANGER
- SURPRISE
- FEAR

A FEW THINGS NOT TO DO WHEN YOU ARE GRIEVING.....

1. LIVE IN THE PAST
2. REFUSE TO MAKE THE CHANGES TO MOVE FORWARD
3. DWELL IN SELF- PITY
4. LOSE RESPECT FOR YOU AS A HUMAN BEING
5. RUNAWAY FROM YOUR FEELINGS
6. RELY ON DRUGS OR ALCOHOL

PONDER THE MOMENT
"LUKE 2:19"

PONDER THE MOMENT
"LUKE 2:19"

PONDER THE MOMENT
"LUKE 2:19"

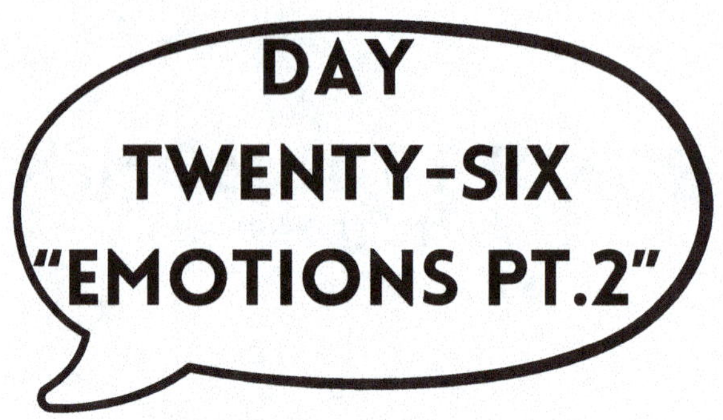

I WOKE UP FEELING

 AWESOME  GOOD  OKAY  NOT GOOD  HORRIBLE

YOUR EMOTIONS CAN BE EXPRESSED THROUGH TONE OF
VOICE,
BODY LANGUAGE, AND FACIAL EXPRESSION.
SOMETIME WE USE A MASK TO COVER UP
HOW WE ARE ACTUALLY FEELING.
WEARING A MASK IS SO MUCH SAFER, BUT IS NOT
BENEFICIAL FOR THE HEALING PROCESS.
THE LONGER YOU WEAR A MASK FOR YOUR EMOTION,
THE LONGER IT TAKES TO HEAL.
THE CHOICE IS YOURS......
..........COVERING YOUR EMOTIONS IS NOT OKAY..........

WRITE DOWN ONE EMOTION THAT YOU CAN WORK ON
AND WHY.

PHILIPPIANS 4:4
"REJOICE IN THE LORD ALWAY: AND AGAIN I SAY, REJOICE."

PONDER THE MOMENT
"LUKE 2:19"

PONDER THE MOMENT
"LUKE 2:19"

PONDER THE MOMENT
"LUKE 2:19"

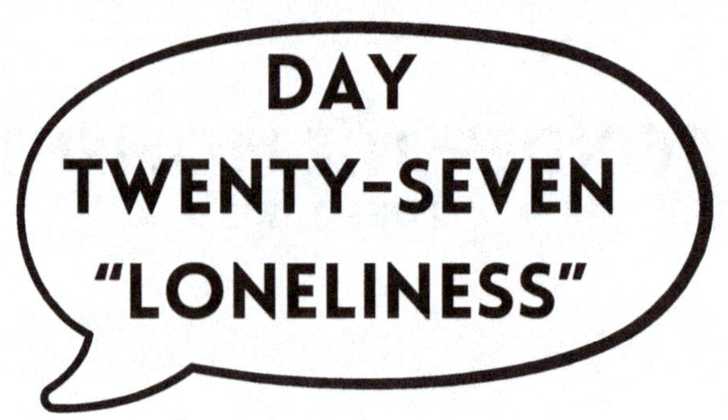

I WOKE UP FEELING

AWESOME **GOOD** **OKAY** **NOT GOOD** **HORRIBLE**

DEFINE LONELINESS–

____

____

7TIPS TO COPE WITH LONELINESS
1.GET AROUND PEOPLE WHO KNOW GRIEF
THEY CAN RELATE AND WALK WITH YOU
2.TAKE CARE OF YOURSELF(EAT, SLEEP, EXERCISE)
3.RELEASE YOUR EXPECTATIONS
4.FORGIVE YOURSELF AND OTHERS
(LET GO OF THE GUILT AND BITTERNESS)
5.LIMIT YOUR TIME WITH NEGATIVE PEOPLE
6.FIND HEALTHY WAYS TO COPE WITH YOUR LONELINESS
(CRY, TALK, MEDITATE ,JOURNAL)
7.BALANCE YOUR TIME

WHAT HAS HELPED YOU DEAL WITH LONELINESS IN A POSITIVE WAY?

HAVE YOU FELT ALONE IN YOUR GRIEF JOURNEY?
YES OR NO

PONDER THE MOMENT
"LUKE 2:19"

PONDER THE MOMENT
"LUKE 2:19"

PONDER THE MOMENT
"LUKE 2:19"

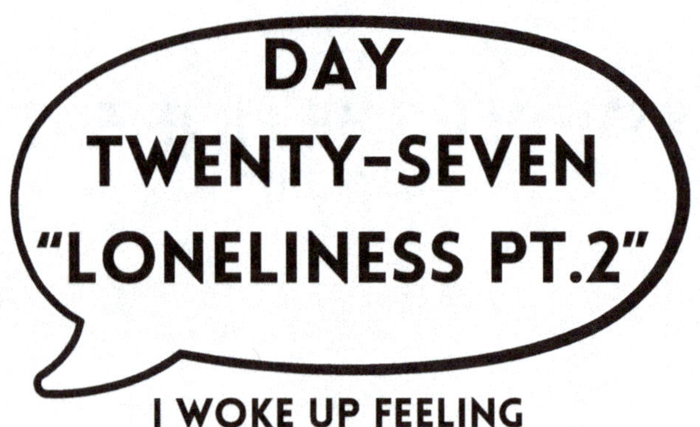

I WOKE UP FEELING

 AWESOME  GOOD  OKAY  NOT GOOD  HORRIBLE

WHAT DOES IT EVEN MEAN TO BE LONELY
AFTER A LOVE ONE HAS PASSED AWAY?
WE ALL HAVE THAT DESIRE TO SHUT THE WORLD OUT AND
RETREAT TO AN UNKNOWN OR FAMILIAR PLACE TO BE
ALONE TO CRY, TO SCREAM,
OR TO BLAME OURSELVES, OR EVEN QUESTION OUR OWN
EXISTENCE.
UNASHAMEDLY I HAVE BEEN TO THAT PLACE MANY TIMES.
JUST KNOW YOU ARE NOT ALONE AND NEVER HAVE BEEN.
EVEN WHEN WE THINK GOD ISN'T THERE HE IS.

WHAT IS SOMETHING THAT YOU CAN DO TO HELP YOU FEEL LESS
LONELY?

HEBREWS 13:5
"LET YOUR CONVERSATION BE WITHOUT COVETOUSNESS; AND BE
CONTENT WITH SUCH THINGS AS YE HAVE: FOR HE HATH SAID,
I WILL NEVER LEAVE THEE, NOR FORSAKE THEE."

PONDER THE MOMENT
"LUKE 2:19"

PONDER THE MOMENT
"LUKE 2:19"

PONDER THE MOMENT
"LUKE 2:19"

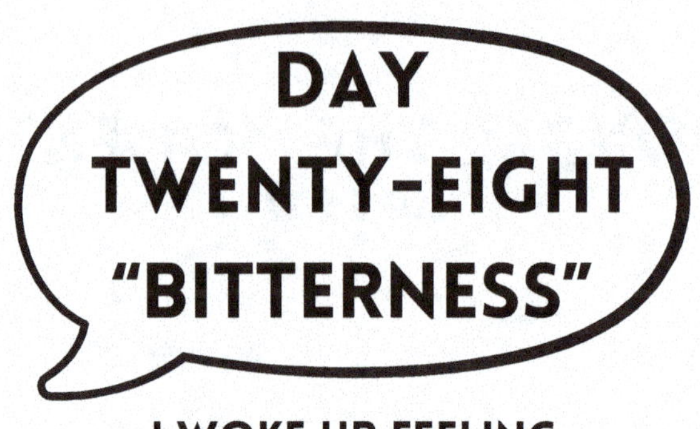

I WOKE UP FEELING

AWESOME　　GOOD　　OKAY　　NOT GOOD　　HORRIBLE

BITTERNESS-
ANGER AND DISAPPOINTMENT AT BEING TREATED
UNFAIRLY; RESENTMENT

WHAT DOES BITTERNESS MEAN TO YOU?

IF YOU FIND YOURSELF AT BITTERNESS'S DOOR:
HERE ARE SOME TIPS TO HELP RELEASE BITTERNESS!!
1.PRACTICE EMPATHY.
2.REFLECT ON TIMES WHEN OTHERS HAVE FORGIVEN YOU.
3.PRAY AND PRAY FOR OTHERS.
4.LET GO AND LET GOD TAKE OVER.

HOW HAS BITTERNESS AFFECTED OR NOT AFFECTED YOU IN YOUR GRIEF JOURNEY?

IF YOU ARE NOT FORGIVING, BITTERNESS WILL SET IN. IN MY OPINION BITTERNESS IS LIKE YOU DRINKING POISON AND HOPING THE OTHER PERSON DIE 😬.

PONDER THE MOMENT
"LUKE 2:19"

PONDER THE MOMENT
"LUKE 2:19"

PONDER THE MOMENT
"LUKE 2:19"

____

____

____

____

____

____

____

____

____

____

____

____

____

____

____

____

____

____

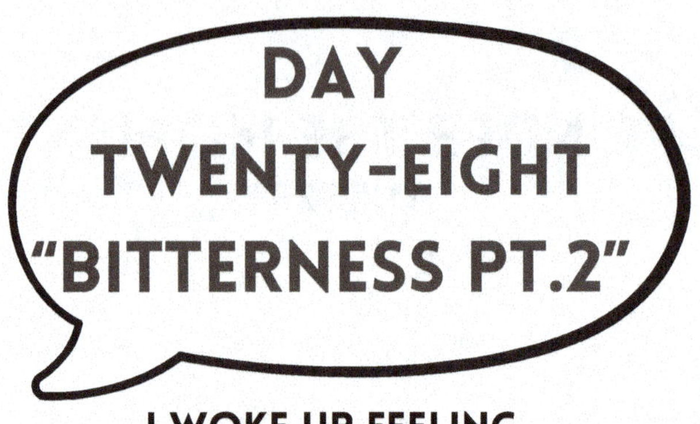

I WOKE UP FEELING

 AWESOME    GOOD    OKAY    NOT GOOD    HORRIBLE

CAN BITTERNESS CHANGE A PERSON? YES / NO

.IF YOU ARE NOT FORGIVING, BITTERNESS WILL SET IN. FOR ME BITTERNESS IS LIKE YOU DRINKING POISON AND HOPING THE OTHER PERSON DIE 😬. REGARDLESS OF THE SITUATION WE HAVE TO LET IT DIE OR IT WILL KILL US FROM THE INSIDE OUT.

DEPRESSION ARRIVES WHEN YOU LOSE HOPE!!

WHAT CAN YOU DO PERSONALLY TO LET GO OF BITTERNESS?

WHAT ARE OTHER WAYS THAT CAN GUIDE YOU AWAY FROM BITTERNES?

EPHESIANS 4:31
"LET ALL BITTERNESS, AND WRATH, AND ANGER, AND CLAMOUR, AND EVIL SPEAKING, BE PUT AWAY FROM YOU, WITH ALL MALICE:"

PONDER THE MOMENT
"LUKE 2:19"

PONDER THE MOMENT
"LUKE 2:19"

PONDER THE MOMENT
"LUKE 2:19"

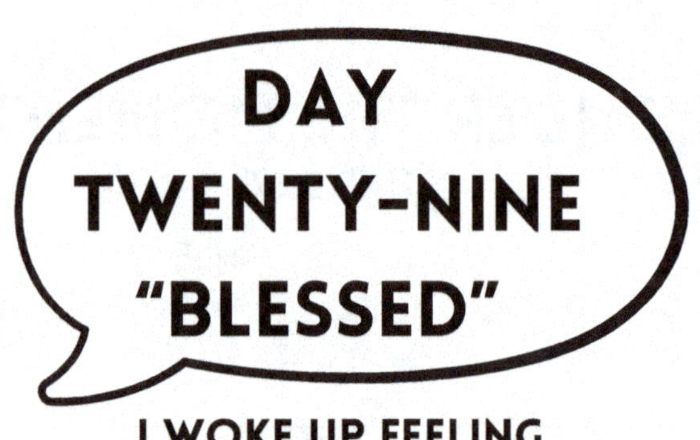

I WOKE UP FEELING

 AWESOME  GOOD  OKAY  NOT GOOD  HORRIBLE

DEFINE - BLESSED

____

____

Blessed!

"BLESSED ARE THOSE THAT MOURN FOR THEY SHALL BE COMFORTED. JESUS HAS TAUGHT US AND HIS DISCIPLES AS WELL TO TAKE COMFORT IN KNOWING, THAT WE WILL BE BLESSED WHEN WE SUFFER. JESUS ALSO REMINDS US THAT SUFFERING AND BLESSINGS ARE CONNECTED.
THE MEANING OF BLESS- IS TO ASK FOR GOD'S HELP AND PROTECTION FOR SOMEONE OR SOMETHIN.

"4 TYPES OF BLESSINGS FROM GOD"

DIVINE PROSPERITY   FRUITFULNESS

DIVINE HEALTH   LONG LIFE

3 WAYS TO BE BLESSED
KEEP GOD'S COMMANDMENTS
BE A BLESSING TO OTHERS
HONOR YOUR PARENTS (IF THEY ARE STILL ALIVE)

PONDER THE MOMENT
"LUKE 2:19"

PONDER THE MOMENT
"LUKE 2:19"

PONDER THE MOMENT
"LUKE 2:19"

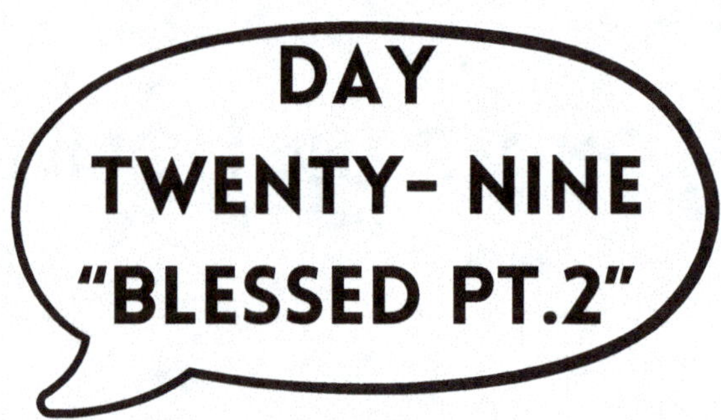

I WOKE UP FEELING

AWESOME **GOOD** **OKAY** **NOT GOOD** **HORRIBLE**

TO BE BLESSED MEANS TO BE FAVORED BY GOD

HOW CAN YOU BE A BLESSING TO THOSE AROUND YOU?

WHAT IS YOUR GREATEST BLESSING FROM GOD?

WHAT ARE SOME DAILY BLESSINGS IN YOUR LIFE?

ROMANS 5:8
"BUT GOD COMMENDETH HIS LOVE TOWARD US, IN THAT, WHILE WE WERE YET SINNERS, CHRIST DIED FOR US."

PONDER THE MOMENT
"LUKE 2:19"

PONDER THE MOMENT
"LUKE 2:19"

PONDER THE HEART
"LUKE 2:19"

I WOKE UP FEELING

 AWESOME
 GOOD
 OKAY
 NOT GOOD
 HORRIBLE

......YOUR STORY IS NOT OVER.....
.......IT'S JUST BEGINNING.......

IN YOUR OWN WORDS WHAT IS YOUR NEXT STEP IN YOUR GRIEF JOURNEY?

DO YOU TRUST GOD AND KEEP LIVING OR DO YOU JUST GIVE UP? (DON'T GIVE UP KEEP MOVING)

YES OR NO

-TIPS TO MOVE FORWARD BECAUSE YOU DEFINITELY CAN-
SET ACHIEVABLE GOALS (HAVE SOMETHING YOU CAN WORK TOWARD)
STAY CONNECTED (MAINTAIN A RELATIONSHIP WITH FAMILY AND FRIENDS)
PLEASE BE PATIENT WITH YOURSELF (HEALING IS A SLOW STEADY PROCESS) TAKE YOUR TIME!
JOHN 14:3
"AND IF I GO AND PREPARE A PLACE FOR YOU, I WILL COME AGAIN, AND RECEIVE YOU UNTO MYSELF; THAT WHERE I AM, THERE YE MAY BE ALSO."

PONDER THE HEART
"LUKE 2:19"

PONDER THE HEART
"LUKE 2:19"

PONDER THE HEART
"LUKE 2:19"

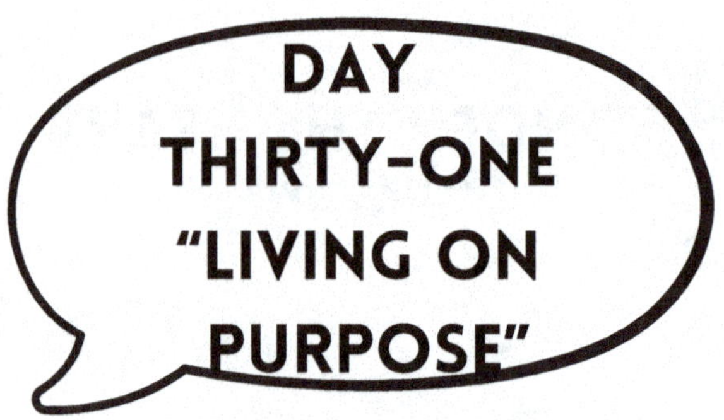

I WOKE UP FEELING

 AWESOME  GOOD  OKAY  NOT GOOD  HORRIBLE

CELEBRATE THE SMALL VICTORIES ON PURPOSE .....

AS A BEREAVED PARENT, I KNOW THE STRUGGLE OF
MOVING FORWARD
WHEN PART OF OUR FAMILY IS MISSING.
THE MERE THOUGHT OF MOVING FORWARD
SCARES MOST OF US, AND THAT'S OK.
ONE THING THAT BRINGS COMFORT IS
KNOWING THAT EVERYDAY WITHOUT OUR LOVED ONES
IS ONE DAY CLOSER TO SEEING THEM AGAIN.
TODAY, WE CELEBRATE THE SMALL VICTORIES IN OUR LIFE....
(YOU KNOW THE ONES ONLY YOU AND GOD SEE)
TODAY, WE LIVE OUR LIFE ON PURPOSE....
TODAY, WE WILL BE HAPPY ON PURPOSE....
TODAY, WE TAKE ANOTHER STEP FORWARD ON PURPOSE....

"TIPS ON HOW TO MOVE FORWARD IN LIFE AFTER DEATH"
GIVE YOURSELF PERMISSION TO BE HAPPY....
COME TO TERMS WITH A NEW NORMAL....
GRIEF WILL ALWAYS BE THERE, BUT IT DOESN'T HAVE TO RULE
YOUR LIFE....
YOU ARE NOT RESPONSIBLE FOR HOW OTHERS FEEL ABOUT
YOUR GRIEF....
MOVING FORWARD DOESN'T MEAN YOU ARE FORGETTING
THEM....

PONDER THE HEART
"LUKE 2:19"

PONDER THE HEART
"LUKE 2:19"

PONDER THE MOMENT
"LUKE 2:19"

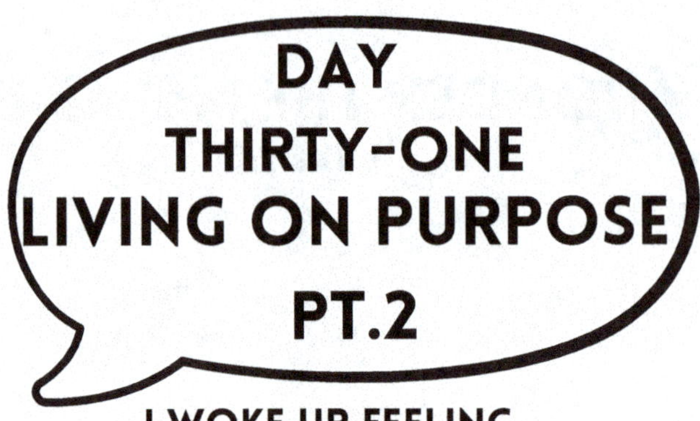

I WOKE UP FEELING

AWESOME **GOOD** **OKAY** **NOT GOOD** **HORRIBLE**

CELEBRATE THE SMALL VICTORIES ON PURPOSE .....

PICK A PICTURE THAT MADE YOU HAPPY ON PURPOSE
AND TALK ABOUT IT!!!

____

____

____

____

ISAIAH 55:8
**"FOR MY THOUGHTS ARE NOT YOUR THOUGHTS, NEITHER
ARE YOUR WAYS MY WAYS, SAITH THE LORD."**

PONDER THE MOMENT
"LUKE 2:19"

PONDER THE MOMENT
"LUKE 2:19"

I AM NO STRANGER TO GRIEF. AS I WAS PUTTING THIS BOOK TOGETHER, EVERY CHAPTER HAS HELPED ME TO BECOME A BIT STRONGER IN MY WALK THROUGH GRIEF. MY ONLY HOPE IS THAT YOU ALLOWED GOD TO GUIDE YOU THROUGH THIS BOOK, AND ALLOW HIM TO CONTINUE TO WALK BESIDE YOU IN THE DAYS AHEAD. ONE THING TO REMEMBER AFTER YOU FINISH THIS DEVOTIONAL IS THAT GRIEF IS VERY REAL. GRIEF SHOWS UP WHEN IT WANTS. YOU CAN'T SCHEDULE IT, YOU CAN'T HIDE FROM IT, OR DRINK IT AWAY. GRIEF WILL WAIT FOR YOU. WHEN GRIEF COMES, AND IT WILL, ALLOW IT TO COME INSIDE AND HAVE A SEAT WITH YOU.
BECOME ONE WITH YOUR GRIEF

YOURS TRULY,
LAWANDA WALKER-TAVE

ARE YOU IN NEED OF A CHRISTIAN COUNSELOR TO HELP YOU NAVIGATE THROUGH
LIFE STORMS AND STRUGGLES?
I HIGHLY RECOMMEND LEGENDARY CONSULTING.
GET HELP FOR WHATEVER NEEDS HELP!!!

www.ingramcontent.com/pod-product-compliance
Lightning Source LLC
Chambersburg PA
CBHW070858160726
48004CB00003B/1140